This book belongs to ...

_____

THE ACTION BIBLE

Easter

25 Stories about Jesus' Resurrection

DAVID C COOK

transforming lives together

THE ACTION BIBLE EASTER
Published by David C Cook
4050 Lee Vance Drive
Colorado Springs, CO 80918 U.S.A.

Integrity Music Limited, a Division of David C Cook
Brighton, East Sussex BN1 2RE, England

The graphic circle C logo is a registered trademark of David C Cook.

Library of Congress Control Number 2022938216
ISBN 978-0-8307-8466-0
eISBN 978-0-8307-8467-7

© 2023 David C Cook
Illustrations © 2023 Sergio Cariello Studio, Inc.

The Team: Amy Konyndyk, Stephanie Bennett, Judy Gillispie, Parker
Bennett, Vicki Kuyper, James Hershberger, Susan Murdock
Cover Design: James Hershberger

Printed in Canada
First Edition 2023

1 2 3 4 5 6 7 8 9 10

080822

Contents

The Easter Story

Mark 15:12–47; 16:1–7

"What shall I do, then, with the one you call the king of the Jews?" Pilate asked them.

"Crucify him!" they shouted.

"Why? What crime has he committed?" asked Pilate.

But they shouted all the louder, "Crucify him!"

Wanting to satisfy the crowd, Pilate released Barabbas to them. He had Jesus flogged, and handed him over to be crucified.

The soldiers led Jesus away into the palace (that is, the Praetorium) and called together the whole company of soldiers. They put a purple robe on him, then twisted together a crown of thorns and set it on him. And they began to call out to him, "Hail, king of the Jews!" Again and again they struck him on the head with a staff and spit on him. Falling on their knees, they paid homage to him. And when they had mocked him, they took off the purple robe and put his own clothes on him. Then they led him out to crucify him.

A certain man from Cyrene, Simon, the father of Alexander and Rufus, was passing by on his way in from the country, and they forced him to carry the cross. They brought Jesus to the place called Golgotha (which means "the place of the skull"). Then they offered him wine mixed with myrrh, but he did not take it. And they crucified him. Dividing up his clothes, they cast lots to see what each would get.

It was nine in the morning when they crucified him. The written notice of the charge against him read: THE KING OF THE JEWS.

They crucified two rebels with him, one on his right and one on his left. Those who passed by hurled insults at him, shaking their heads and saying, "So! You who are going to destroy the temple and build it in three days, come down from the cross and save yourself!" In the same way the chief priests and the teachers of the law mocked him among themselves. "He saved others," they said, "but he can't save himself! Let this Messiah, this king of Israel, come down now from the cross, that we may see and believe." Those crucified with him also heaped insults on him.

At noon, darkness came over the whole land until three in the afternoon. And at three in the afternoon Jesus cried out in a loud voice, *"Eloi, Eloi, lema sabachthani?"* (which means "My God, my God, why have you forsaken me?").

When some of those standing near heard this, they said, "Listen, he's calling Elijah."

Someone ran, filled a sponge with wine vinegar, put it on a staff, and offered it to Jesus to drink. "Now leave him alone. Let's see if Elijah comes to take him down," he said.

With a loud cry, Jesus breathed his last.

The curtain of the temple was torn in two from top to bottom. And when the centurion, who stood there in front of Jesus, saw how he died, he said, "Surely this man was the Son of God!"

Some women were watching from a distance. Among them were Mary Magdalene, Mary the mother of James the younger and of Joseph, and Salome. In Galilee these women had followed him and cared for his needs. Many other women who had come up with him to Jerusalem were also there.

It was Preparation Day (that is, the day before the Sabbath). So as evening approached, Joseph of Arimathea, a prominent member of the Council, who was himself waiting for the kingdom of God, went boldly to Pilate and asked for Jesus' body. Pilate was surprised to hear that he was already dead. Summoning the centurion, he asked him if Jesus had already died. When he learned from the centurion that it was so, he gave the body to Joseph. So Joseph bought some linen cloth, took down the body, wrapped it in the linen, and placed it in a tomb cut out of rock. Then he rolled a stone against the entrance of the tomb. Mary Magdalene and Mary the mother of Joseph saw where he was laid.

When the Sabbath was over, Mary Magdalene, Mary the mother of James, and Salome bought spices so that they might go to anoint Jesus' body. Very early on the first day of the week, just after sunrise, they were on their way to the tomb and they asked each other, "Who will roll the stone away from the entrance of the tomb?"

But when they looked up, they saw that the stone, which was very large, had been rolled away. As they entered the tomb, they saw a young man dressed in a white robe sitting on the right side, and they were alarmed.

"Don't be alarmed," he said. "You are looking for Jesus the Nazarene, who was crucified. He has risen! He is not here. See the place where they laid him. But go, tell his disciples and Peter, 'He is going ahead of you into Galilee. There you will see him, just as he told you.'"

† † †

1

Bartimaeus

The very first thing I ever saw was Jesus' face. It was a kind face. I'd been blind since the day I was born and had never seen a smile before. But I knew right away what the look on His face had to mean. It meant He didn't see me as just another blind beggar along the road. He saw me as a person, as someone who mattered enough for Him to stop and heal. That means more to me than I can ever really put into words.

The minute I heard that Jesus, the teacher and miracle worker, was going to pass my way, I knew I had to plead with Him for help. I knew He was my only chance to see the world around me. If only I could see, I wouldn't need to beg. I could work like other men. I could help others instead of always having to depend on them to help me. It would change my *life*!

So when I heard Jesus coming near, I began crying out at the top of my lungs, asking for His help and mercy. I shouted as loudly as I could, trying to be heard above the noise of the crowd. People nearby told me to hush. "Be quiet, Bartimaeus!" they hissed, like I was some disobedient child.

I think they were embarrassed by how loudly I was yelling. Honestly, I was a little surprised at myself. For years I've sat quietly, making as little trouble as possible. I typically find shade somewhere on the side of the road. Every day, I've waited silently for someone to place a coin in my open, empty hand. Then I can buy food that day. That … *sigh* … has been my life.

But not today! Today, Jesus called me to His side. One minute everything was dark. Then Jesus said that my faith had healed me—and the light of the world came streaming into my life! Certainly, a man who has the power to change me in an instant has the power to change the world. That's why I've left the shade of this palm tree. I've left the darkness behind. Today, and tomorrow, and every day from now on, I'm following Jesus, wherever He leads!

If you were blind, what would you miss seeing?

Why do you think Jesus healed the blind beggar?

What kinds of miracles do you think Jesus performs today?

2
Dog

I've enjoyed a lazy morning nap, and the sun is toasty on my fur. I decide to slowly roll over to warm my belly for a while when I notice … I'm so hung*rrr*y. Of course, that's not unusual for a dog who doesn't have a home of his own. That's why I stay by the side of the road that leads to the city of Jerusalem. So many people pass this way each day. Some drop coins into the hands of the beggars. But if I rub up close to the leg of a stranger and give him a sad little puppy-dog smile and wag my tail, sometimes he drops a piece of food for me. Life can be *rrr*uff when you're on your own.

I'm not sure, but I think my name is Down Boy. At least, that's what the people along the road usually call me. And today there seem to be more people than usual! Look! Here comes a whole group of travelers. Some of the young men are laughing and smiling, some look serious, and some push each other like brothers. They smell a bit like fish. Mmm!

One of the men, the leader maybe, stops and begins to tell the others a story, and the rest of the group crowds around to listen. They're paying such close attention to what He's saying that there's probably no chance they'll even notice me. I curl up near the feet of one of the men, my tummy g*rrr*umbling, and close my tired eyes. Then I feel someone pat my head. Not only does he *rrr*uffle the fur under my chin, but he also holds out a piece of bread. I gobble it down before he can change his mind.

Sc*rrr*umptious! The man gives me another pat on the head, and a friendly smile, and then rejoins his group of friends because they're starting to walk again. I watch as they continue down the road. Other people are starting to gather with the storyteller and the bread man as they all head out. I'm not sure why, but I feel like I should do the same. I get up, give my dusty fur a shake, and trot along with the crowd toward the big city. There's adventure ahead! I can just smell it. Just like I sense there's something g*rrr*eat about that storyteller—and it's more than just bread.

Why do you think God made dogs?

Do you think God cares about animals? Why or why not?

What can we learn from animals?

3
Martha

I was working as fast as I could, trying to get everything ready for dinner. The goats had to be milked. Bread had to be baked. The lamb had to be roasted. Fruit had to be gathered. The humble home I share with my sister, Mary, and brother, Lazarus, still needed tidying.

My hands were moving as fast as my racing mind. But then I stopped and took a deep breath. I remembered what Jesus told me the last time He and His friends visited us. Jesus reminded me that the things I was so worried about were small things, not big ones. The big thing, the most important thing, is growing closer to God. As usual, He's so wise!

Glancing out the window, I see Jesus and His twelve friends just down the road—and it looks like a skinny little dog has decided to join them! I place the dried figs I bought at the market into a bowl. I'd planned to chop some almonds and then walk down to the vineyard and gather some grapes as well. But figs will do for now. Our guests will be here any minute! I pick up the bowl of fruit and a pitcher of fresh water. Then I grab a lamb bone for the dog. I might as well make everyone feel welcome!

Truthfully, Jesus and His followers feel more like family than guests. They're always welcome here. They see so many things in their travels; they meet so many people. I love listening to Jesus tell His stories. He always gives me something to think about. He has such a way of making me feel like I'm a member of God's family: wanted, loved, and understood. After spending time with Him, I want to share God's love with others so they feel that way too.

Tomorrow, meals will need to be prepared and my home will need cleaning all over again. But who knows when Jesus will return for a visit? At this moment—this very special moment—Jesus is almost within arm's reach. I can't imagine anything I'd rather do or any place I'd rather be than sitting at His feet and listening to Him speak once more.

What is your favorite food?

What can you do to make a guest feel at home?

What is one way you can grow closer to God?

4
Matthew

It's been amazing to travel with Jesus as one of His disciples. Watching Jesus teach people and perform miracles has opened my eyes to the wonders of God's power. But if I'm being honest, I'm a little nervous about traveling to Jerusalem.

Don't get me wrong! I trust Jesus with my life, and I am so grateful for the compassion He has shown me. Before I met Him, I was a tax collector working for the Roman Empire. A lot of people thought I was a traitor for helping an empire that oppresses God's people. Then one day, Jesus came to me and called me to be one of His disciples. I was so excited that I quit my job and left everything behind to follow Him. Ever since then, I've lived my life alongside the other disciples, and I go wherever they go.

But Jerusalem? Surely Jesus has heard the rumors: the Pharisees and priests there are furious with Him for performing miracles and declaring Himself the Son of God. I've even heard talk that the Pharisees are willing to work with the Romans to put an end to Jesus' ministry. I hope He realizes the danger He's in.

Why can't we continue teaching throughout the rest of Israel? Jesus has already healed so many people and led many more to follow Him. Why not keep teaching and saving those who are lost? Why must we go to the place where we are despised the most? Jesus has told us before that He will be delivered into the hands of the high priest and sentenced to die. Why doesn't He avoid that fate? Is He *trying* to get Himself killed?

All I know is that the Romans are brutal when it comes to putting people on trial. If Jesus gets into trouble, it will be very hard to set Him free. Maybe He'll change His mind and go somewhere else. Then again, I've never once seen Jesus go back on what He says He'll do.

I spoke to Mark and Luke about it, and they agree that going to Jerusalem seems like a risky idea. But not Peter. He said he would follow Jesus anywhere—even to His death. I pray it doesn't come to that.

Who makes you feel brave?

If you were Matthew, would you be worried about going to Jerusalem? Why or why not?

What risky thing have you ever felt like God was asking you to do?

5
Colt

Being a young colt usually isn't very exciting, so that's why today was extra special!

I've always lived in a little town near Jerusalem. We see travelers passing by, but otherwise, it's often quiet. I just stand around, eating hay and watching people come and go. It may sound kind of boring, but not to me. I enjoy the slow, easy life of a young donkey.

But today … *hee-haw*! It all started when two men with friendly eyes and pleasant voices came up and started untying me from my post. I was a bit curious at first, especially when my owner came out and asked the men what they were doing. But then they said something very unexpected: the Lord needed me.

Really? The Lord needed *me*? I was so surprised! Who is the Lord? And what could He want with a little colt like me? Still, I was determined to be useful, so I eagerly trotted along with the men.

After a short walk, they brought me to their teacher. They called Him Jesus. He was very kind to me. He gently tickled my big ears—*hee-haw*—while His followers placed their cloaks on my back for Him to sit on. Then the teacher climbed onto me, and we all set off toward Jerusalem.

I still wasn't sure who this mysterious teacher Jesus was, but I was beginning to get the idea He was important. Was He a king in disguise? I walked very slowly as we made our way toward the city. I had never carried a person on my back before, and I wanted to do everything right!

As we got close to Jerusalem and passed through the gate, there was a huge crowd waiting for us. All the people—men, women, children—began throwing their cloaks down for the teacher and me to walk across. Some people cut down palm leaves and began waving them as a sign of respect for Jesus. Everyone was praising Him, shouting "Hosanna" as we passed through the crowded streets. It was the most amazing thing. I couldn't help but hold my head a little higher. I'm so glad God wanted me to be a small part of it!

Do you live in more of a quiet little village (like where the donkey was found) or a large, busy city (like Jerusalem)?

What was the donkey's attitude when the men needed him?

How can you prepare for what God may have for your future?

6
Child on Palm Sunday

A king is coming! A king is coming! At least, that's what everyone around me is saying. I've never seen a king before. I wonder if He'll wear a crown covered in jewels. Maybe He's traveling through Jerusalem's streets on a throne, carried by His servants! He might even carry a golden sword, ready to fight for the Jews, for people like my family and me. One thing I *do* know for sure: since He's a king, He'll be strong and powerful. But I wonder if He'll be kind. I wonder if He'd even notice a little girl like me.

It's hard for me to see anything with so many grown-ups crowded all around me. I'm only six and not very big for my age. So instead of trying to stand up tall, I squat down and push my way through a sea of legs and robes toward the front of the crowd. The cries all around me are getting louder. People are shouting, "Hosanna! Save us!" The king must be getting closer.

I squeeze past the knees of a large, bald-headed man who's thrown his coat in the road to honor the king. I excitedly peek my head out from the crowd and look down the road. But all I see is an ordinary man riding on a donkey. The man's dark hair is hanging long and free, and His robes and sandaled feet are dirty from dust on the road. Certainly, this can't be Him! But people are waving palm branches and tossing them in His path. That's a sign of joy and victory! This must be Him. The king of the Jews, the man they call Jesus, the Messiah.

I have to admit, I'm kind of disappointed. I don't see a jewel or flash of gold anywhere. But then the king looks my way. His eyes briefly connect with mine, and His smile is somehow gentle and yet brighter than the shiniest gold I can imagine. The king sees *me*! He's looking at me the way my own *Abba* Daddy does. Even though we've never met, somehow this king makes me feel loved. Hosannas and other praises pour from my lips, just like water from our well, as the *Abba* King passes by. Maybe He will save us!

How do you think the people felt that day seeing Jesus enter Jerusalem?

What do we expect from kings and queens? Why?

What do you think Jesus thought of the crowds?

Pharisee

Here comes that "Jesus of Nazareth," passing through the gates of our city like a king. He must love all the attention from the cheering people. And then, He proclaims Himself to be the Son of God! Clearly, this Jesus is a fraud. I should know; I'm one of the Pharisees!

When it comes to the people who follow God's Word, we're the best of the best. We know all the correct prayers, we can recite entire passages of Scripture, and we make sure to keep ourselves holy and pure to impress God and earn His favor. And yet Jesus is merely a carpenter. Did He study in the temple for years and years the way I did? I think not!

Jesus spends most of His time teaching common people and visiting their homes. Doesn't He know those people are impure?! Why does He choose to be around them? If He were a *real* teacher—like me—He would spend His days in the temple, seeking counsel and wisdom from the priests and elders. Instead, He wastes His time trying to befriend thieves, the diseased, and tax collectors! Why, it doesn't make any sense!

Oh my, it gets worse … They *say* Jesus has been performing miracles. How could they be so easily fooled?! Whether it's true or not, the people have taken these as proof that He is the Son of God. How can Jesus do all this without seeking our approval? We know best!

As if all of that weren't bad enough, some people have started referring to Jesus as the Messiah. *Seriously?!* How can they honestly think Jesus is the promised Messiah? He can't be! The *true* Messiah will appear in glory and majesty, coming down from heaven, not as this common carpenter, riding on a donkey!

Now these people are waving palm leaves at Him and calling for Him to save them. If this goes on, people may turn away from us and start following Jesus instead. He must be stopped! Perhaps the Romans can help us get rid of this Jesus once and for all. We have to restore order and get back to the old ways. We know the laws and the way things have always been. Once things are quiet again—whatever it takes—the people will thank us.

When have you ever felt jealous of someone? How did you deal with it?

How might the Pharisees have responded to Jesus' message of loving your enemies?

In what ways were the Pharisees confused about why Jesus came?

8
Temple Merchant

I think I'm going to have to find a new way to make a living.

A little while ago, I was sitting at my stall in the temple. It was like any other day. I was selling doves so people could offer them to God to be cleansed of their sins. Best prices, cleanest doves! Yeah, I know—the chaos and noise of bartering and exchanging money is a little weird in what should be a holy place, but hey, it's more convenient for all of us than standing outside the temple gates. Besides, no one's ever outright told us merchants we *couldn't* offer our services in that spot.

So anyway, there I was, conducting my usual business, when a man named Jesus walked in. Suddenly, He got really angry! He ran at us and started flipping over our tables, yelling, and telling us to get out. Before I knew what was happening, He got to my area! He turned over my bench, and in my hurry to get out of His way, I knocked my cage of birds to the ground. The cage broke, and all my doves flew away! Now *I* was the one who was outraged; I could've made some good money selling those doves!

Eventually, He chased all the merchants away. It left quite a mess! People were shocked. I continued to quietly watch from behind a table as I scraped up the few scattered coins I could find. Jesus began to calm down. He still seemed angry, but I could tell that He was also sad.

A few Pharisees asked Him what He was doing. Jesus told them it was wrong for us to be trading things in the temple. He said that we were dishonoring God's holy temple and that we had turned His Father's house into a place that welcomed thieves.

I was still thinking about what happened as I was walking home later. I wasn't expecting to feel bad when He said that, but for some reason, I did. Maybe it *was* wrong to be selling things in the temple. After all, it's supposed to be a place to worship God, not to try to make money.

Maybe I should go find Jesus and learn more. I'm curious to know why He did what He did when others have been fine with it for so long. Who is He? Maybe it's time for me to make a change in my life.

† † †

Is it strange to imagine Jesus getting so angry? Why or why not?

Why was Jesus the only one who was upset with the merchants?

What other things do you think make Jesus sad or angry?

9
Judas

I feel the weight of the thirty silver coins in my hands. It feels good. If I worked in a regular trade, as a carpenter or a stonecutter, this would be two months' wages. Instead, I'm following a teacher named Jesus around the countryside, depending on the charity of people we meet to provide us food and shelter. This is the first money I've had to call my own in months.

Of course, as the treasurer, I look after the little bit of money our small group of men receives now and then. Sure, I've helped myself to a few coins once or twice. No one's ever noticed. Not that Jesus really cares about money anyway. He shares what little we have with needy strangers.

Once He even praised a woman who, instead of washing His feet with water, used expensive perfume. That perfume was worth a year's salary! I think Jesus would just as soon give away the little money we have than use it to buy better food or a new cloak. Sometimes I don't understand what He values at all.

The only thing I had to do to earn these coins was provide a little information. The religious leaders asked me where Jesus would be tonight. So I told them. After our meal, I'll point Him out to them, and then my job's done. What they do after that is of no concern to me. He's the one who decided to return to Jerusalem, knowing the danger.

Right now, I'd better hurry or I'll be late for Passover supper with Jesus and the others. I wonder if He already knows what I've done … He's kind of funny that way. I feel like He knows me better than I know myself. He knows how uncomfortable I was with how He handled the merchants at the temple. Even though I disagreed, we've all been through a lot together.

Huh … Jesus is so *forgiving* of the sins of others. I wonder if He will still love me when He learns what I did …

I drop the coins back into the money bag I keep securely tied around my waist and uneasily climb the steps to the upper room. As I push open the door to where we'll dine together, the bag hangs heavy against my hip. Somehow its weight doesn't make me feel as happy as it did before.

Why do you think Judas took the money to betray Jesus and then still went to the supper?

What do you think each disciple was thinking as the group gathered with Jesus?

Has a friend ever done something that hurt you? In what way? Have you ever been that person who hurt someone else?

10
Olive Tree

Come on in. You're welcome to join us here in the garden of Gethsemane. Believe it or not, I'm one of the oldest trees in the grove. I'm 750 years old, give or take a decade. But I'm still going—and growing—even though my trunk is all twisted and knobby.

I come from a long line of olive trees. In fact, I'm sure some of my ancestors even grew in the garden of Eden! God made us not only beautiful but useful too. Our silvery leaves provide shade. Our wood can be used to build chairs or cook meals. Our olives make tasty treats as well as oil for cooking or lighting homes. Did you know that trees like me even help create the air you breathe? God created us trees for all kinds of amazing purposes!

Another unique feature we trees possess is … we're quiet, which makes us *really* good listeners. Tonight, a young man was here asking God for help. Of course, I listened. Not because I'm nosy, but because the man was crying and praying with such urgency. I wanted to help.

While Jesus (that's what His friends called Him) was praying right beneath my branches, do you know what His friends did? They fell asleep! Even after He'd asked them to pray with Him. This must have made Him feel completely alone. Later in the night, another man arrived and greeted Jesus with a kiss on the cheek. Immediately, a noisy group of soldiers showed up and roughly took Jesus away. Those friends who came with Jesus were fully awake then! They scattered like the little creatures that run around the grove at night.

I wanted to do something, but the roots that keep me growing also keep me in one place. I'm sure His friends are praying now, wherever they went. You know, 700 years ago, when I was just a sapling, I heard another man—named Isaiah—talk to God in this garden. I think he was praying about Jesus, the very same man here tonight! (I told you I was a good listener.)

God has a plan. And having known God for as long as I have, I bet it's a good one!

What do you like best about trees?

Why do you think Jesus was crying out as He prayed?

Where is your favorite place to pray? Do you think it makes any difference to God where you are when you pray?

11
Fire in the Courtyard

I begin with a tiny spark. But feed me, and I'll continue to grow. I can leap, dance, crackle, and smolder. A fire's life may be brief, but it's powerful. So don't get too close. I can warm your hands or burn your fingers. I can bake your bread or blacken your toast. I can light up the darkness so you can read or turn your entire home to ash. I can be both your friend and your enemy—hotheaded, moody, and unpredictable.

I guess you could say I'm an awful lot like people. They can warm you with a hug or burn you with their words. Like that man over there, the one now weeping in the shadows. Thanks to my bright-orange light blazing in the high priest's courtyard, I've seen everything that's happened tonight.

Earlier, I watched the soldiers roughly bring in a man named Jesus. They treated Him terribly, made fun of Him, and yanked Him into the palace to see the high priest. The hiding man came in soon after Him, head down, like he wanted to see what was happening but also stay away from the crowd.

A servant girl who'd stopped to warm her hands by my flames said she'd seen him—the one who was trying to hide—with Jesus. The man protested she was mistaken. Another person agreed with her, saying he was certain this man had been one of Jesus' followers. Once again, he denied it was true. This happened yet a third time. By then, he had moved away from my flickering light and into the courtyard's darkest corner. But even there, I could see him clearly. Hot with anger, the man swore he did not know Jesus.

At that moment, the soldiers brought Jesus out of the palace. Although His head was hanging, He lifted it to gaze around the courtyard. As His eyes connected with the hiding man's, a rooster crowed. The soldiers dragged Jesus out through the gates, and that's when the man in the shadows began to weep. Even I could see through the smoke screen of that man's lies. Was the man in the darkness a friend or an enemy? Perhaps, like me, at times he could be both.

Can you name a few good things fire can do?

Why should you never play with fire?

Why do you think Peter, the man who was trying to hide, said he didn't know Jesus?

12

Pilate

As the Roman governor over Judea, my job is to keep the peace and uphold justice. But today was different. Today, I think I may have sentenced an innocent man to die.

There had been reports of uprisings in the land of Judea, and I was sent to enforce Roman authority over the Jewish people—at all costs. Even from my palace, I have heard outcries from the streets below, beyond the high walls. Some Jews defy Rome's authority and wish to be rid of our presence. Such people must be dealt with quickly to serve as an example. If I'm not seen as being in control, the emperor will send someone else who can do the job.

But this man—this Jesus of Nazareth—He is not a rebel. His crime was not one of violence or deceit against Rome. The Jewish priests and elders wish to see Him crucified for declaring Himself to be the Son of God. They gathered a crowd and marched Jesus through the streets to be put on trial outside my palace. The strangest thing was that when I asked Him, Jesus neither defended Himself nor renounced His claim to be God's Son. This made the priests even more furious than before.

From my comfortable seat in the shade, I stared out at the angry crowd that had gathered under the hot sun to watch the trial. As part of a local tradition during this time of year, before sentencing Him, I gave the people the choice of a prisoner whom I would set free. I had hoped they would ask for the release of Jesus, since it didn't seem to me that He had done anything wrong. To my surprise, the crowd instead shouted for the release of another man—a murderer called Barabbas.

My wife then leaned over and warned me not to be involved in Jesus' execution because she'd had a dream and knew He was innocent. With a troubled heart, I asked the crowd what should be done with Jesus. Their answer was clear: "Crucify Him!"

I told the crowd to do what they wanted with Jesus as I washed my hands of it all. I won't be blamed for His death. I don't know if the Hebrew God is real or not, and I don't know exactly who Jesus is, but He is clearly the King of the Jews.

How do you feel when someone gets punished for something they didn't do?

If you had Pilate's power, what would you have said to the angry crowd of people?

What do you wish Jesus had said during His trial?

13
Simon of Cyrene

One slow step at a time, I make my way through the streets of Jerusalem. The wooden cross I'm carrying is so heavy and the streets are so crowded with people that I can't possibly move any faster. Then I look at Jesus, stumbling beside me. It's obvious He's been beaten. There's blood across His body, and someone's crushed a crown of thorns onto His head. He can hardly carry Himself up these cobblestone streets, let alone carry a bulky, splintered cross on His back. That's why the soldiers pulled me from the crowd. They wanted me to carry Jesus' cross for Him.

My name is Simon. But when Jesus fell under the weight of this cross, the soldiers didn't care who I was. The soldier in charge just glared into the crowd, pointed his finger at me, and yelled angrily, "You! Come here!"

I did what I was told. Maybe the soldier chose me because I look strong. I'm no one special. I'm just another Jewish traveler, here in Jerusalem to celebrate the Passover. I was born in North Africa, but when I came into Judea, I began to hear about a man named Jesus, the long-awaited Messiah. I hear that throughout Israel He is helping people find their way back to God.

I left my home in Cyrene with my wife and two sons. We traveled through Egypt, more than a thousand miles, to Israel. We've lived in the countryside for the past few months, where I tried to earn enough money to come to Jerusalem for the Passover.

I'd been hoping to meet Jesus. But not like this.

I'm starting to believe this man is the Messiah—the promised Savior. But still, I'm not quite sure what to think. All I know is that He's hurt and He's suffering. I'm glad the soldier's eyes met mine in the crowd. If I could do anything to help Jesus, I gladly would. It's an honor to carry this heavy cross so Jesus doesn't have to.

The people on either side of us keep pressing closer. They're trying to get a better look at Jesus. Some people are shouting and shaking their fists at us; others are weeping. There's so much noise I can hardly think. But ever so faintly, I hear Jesus praying. So I do the same …

How do you think Jesus felt when Simon carried the cross for Him?

What's the heaviest load you've ever tried to carry, whether physical or emotional?

When you see someone who is struggling on their own, how can you help?

14
Criminal

My life has been one long list of bad choices. I've lied, stolen, cheated, and hurt people. I've cared only about myself—more than I've cared about anyone or anything else in this life. I got away with being greedy, selfish, and cruel for a very long time. But today, my bad choices have finally caught up with me. I'm going to pay for them with my life.

It's too late to change what I've done. But one thing *has* changed: I'm truly sorry for it all. And not just because I got caught. I'm sorry for who I've become. I've wasted the time God gave me. I turned my back on the love my family tried to show me. Although this punishment that Rome has imposed is brutal, I deserve to be here, nailed to this cross to be put to death as punishment for my crimes.

But the man next to me here on this hill—He isn't a criminal. He doesn't deserve this. He's the one the crowds called the Messiah. I've heard the stories … how He's healed the blind and cured the sick. Some say He even raised a man from the dead! His choices have been good ones, loving ones—unlike mine. He's chosen to help people, not hurt them. I don't understand how actions like that could have led Him here.

It's all so unfair! If I were Jesus, I'd be so angry at the people who decided I should die. But He's not. As we walked up this hill, He prayed the whole way. He got it worse than we did—that is, the other criminal and me. He was so weak from being beaten, He couldn't even carry His own cross. Even though He's in pain, He keeps asking God to forgive those who've hurt Him! What kind of man does that?

Jesus walked toward death like He knew exactly where He's going and He's ready. I want to go where He's going. I want the chance to make things right. I want the forgiveness Jesus is offering to those who've hurt Him. If I can get up the courage to talk to such a good, honest man, maybe I'll ask if I can go with Him to heaven. Just imagine if what looks like the end could turn out to be a brand-new beginning!

When you get blamed for something you didn't do, how do you feel?

When someone hurts you, is it hard for you to forgive them? Why or why not?

What did the criminal, who had made bad choices his whole life, see in Jesus? How can you share that with others?

15
James

When Jesus died, many people lost their teacher. But to me, He was more than a teacher. To me, He was my brother.

Even when we were kids, I remember Jesus being different. I looked up to Him in a lot of ways because I was His younger brother, but I began to realize I could never be like Him … and back then, I didn't *want* to be like Him. He was perfect— literally perfect! It was weird growing up with the supposed "Son of God" right in my family.

We didn't talk about it every day or anything, but some people teased me about it, and others said my brother must be crazy. None of that mattered to my mother, Mary. She always knew Jesus was the Messiah—the promised Savior—even if me and my other brothers didn't believe it.

When we all grew up, Jesus left His job as a carpenter helping our dad, Joseph, and began teaching around Galilee. Then He began leading a group of disciples. Not long after that, my family and I started hearing stories that He was performing miracles around Israel. That's when crowds of people really took up following Him around the countryside.

When He finally came home to visit us in Nazareth, my siblings and I were pretty tired of hearing all the talk about Jesus being the Messiah. As we were leaving to go to the festival in Jerusalem, we told Jesus that if He really wanted to be famous, He should go teach the people there. Of course, we were only joking, but Jesus showed up anyway! Once He started teaching, some of the leaders got really mad and tried to grab Him, but somehow He got away. None of us could believe it! He just … disappeared!

A few days ago, when the Romans came to arrest Jesus, He just surrendered to them this time. Why? Why would He do that? Surely He knew what was going to happen! He must've known they were going to …

I wish I had been nicer to Him. I should have respected Him more as my older brother, even if He seemed a little strange at times. I just wish I could tell Him I'm sorry.

What would be fun about growing up with Jesus as your brother?

Why do you think James originally had a hard time believing Jesus was the Messiah?

How do you sincerely apologize to a sibling or a friend?

16

Witness

There were three crucifixions today—each man nailed to a cross as punishment for his crimes. The Romans tend to do a lot of these, and rarely do I feel curious enough to come watch. But this one? None of the ones I've seen have been like this.

The execution began as usual, with the condemned led up the hill, each man carrying his own cross. Like I said, I don't often attend (although many people come and almost seem to enjoy watching), but for some reason, I felt like I was supposed to be there.

Two of the men were murderers found guilty and sentenced to death. But the third man, called Jesus, was accused of calling Himself the Son of God. For that, He was placed between the others to die like a common criminal. I heard Him say, "Father, forgive them, for they do not know what they are doing" (Luke 23:34). The soldiers even took His clothes and divided them up among themselves.

As I stood there, feeling pity for these suffering men, I glanced up at Jesus' face. What I saw there reminded me of going to the synagogue as a young boy; it was as if I could see God's presence in the face of this dying man. I didn't want to watch Him in pain, but I couldn't look away.

The people around me were shouting at Jesus, mocking Him and asking why He didn't save Himself from death. A group of women gathered a little distance away. I could tell they cared for Him. They cried and held each other as they too watched.

Not long after that, the sky started to grow dark, even though it was the middle of the day. The air seemed to change, as if sadness had come over the entire world. My stomach turned as I watched some people lift a sponge of vinegar up to Jesus' lips. After that, He cried out something that I couldn't quite hear … and fell silent.

Without warning, the earth shook and several nearby rocks and stones broke apart. We were terrified! Then everything was still. We all looked at each other in disbelief. Nobody knew what had happened, but we were sure these extraordinary events were no accident. A Roman centurion called out, "Surely this man was the Son of God!" (Mark 15:39).

Later, strange stories spread around Jerusalem: the tombs of the dead had opened, and the temple curtain had torn in two. The more I heard, the more I thought about Jesus. I know all these strange happenings had something to do with His death … but what? Why did He have to die?

What does it mean to be a witness?

What do you know about why Jesus died on the cross? (See page 58 if you want to discuss this now.)

When you don't understand something, who do you ask about it?

17
Priest in the Temple

We priests have received a message from God, but none of us are sure what it means.

This afternoon, deep inside the temple, I was readying myself to burn incense on the altar by the Most Holy Place, where God's presence dwells behind a massive curtain. Even we priests cannot safely pass to the other side of this curtain without a proper ceremony to humble ourselves before the Lord. It is the way we have done things since the time of Moses.

We began the evening sacrifice, as instructed by the law, but this time, something entirely unexpected happened. I've since talked to others who were outside, and they say the sky grew dark far sooner than usual. It was still afternoon, but it appeared to be midnight all across Judea!

Just as I was about to step up to the altar by the heavy curtain separating us from the presence of God, a mighty earthquake struck! The walls of the temple shook. Then suddenly, before my very eyes, the curtain concealing the Most Holy Place tore in two from top to bottom with a fierce ripping sound!

For a moment, I was sure my time had come. *Was I about to die?* I fell to the ground, covered my head, and waited until things quieted. After a time, I slowly opened my eyes. Everything was still again, as if the heavens were expressing a great sorrow. I stared at the curtain, its two halves swaying, revealing the Most Holy Place for all the priests to see. None of us could believe it. How could this be?

Immediately, we began to discuss the meaning of this otherworldly event, but even with all our wisdom, none of us had a clear answer. Was the temple being destroyed from within? Had it lost favor with the Lord? Was God freely welcoming people into His presence?

Did this have anything to do with the death of Jesus of Nazareth, who was said to have died around the same time that the earthquake shook the world? The idea that Jesus may have held favor with God terrified all of us, for some felt responsible for His execution.

Whatever the meaning, one thing is certain: the tearing of the curtain was an act of God, and it holds great significance for all the people of Israel.

How do you think God felt about His Son dying?

When have you seen amazing displays of God's power in nature?

What do you think God was trying to tell the priests by tearing the curtain?

18
Joseph of Arimathea

After what's happened today, I can no longer hide. I've followed Jesus and His teachings for months. But as a member of the Jewish high council, I did this in secret. I didn't want anyone else to know, especially the other Jewish leaders. After all, they're the ones who wanted Jesus dead. They were jealous, and even a bit afraid of Him. Jesus was performing miracles and teaching things they couldn't allow—or understand really. So many people traveled with Him, listening to His teachings. And I'm one of them. But now, Jesus is dead.

I've been a coward. But it's never too late to change and do the right thing. That's why I risked going to Pilate, the Roman governor. Jewish law says a dead body needs to be buried before sunset. Pilate gave me permission to honor that law.

My friend Nicodemus and I worked quickly to take the Messiah's bruised, wounded body down from the cross. Nicodemus, who's a religious leader like me, is also a secret follower of Jesus. Together, we carried Jesus' body to a tomb I'd purchased for my own family, carved into the rocky hillside of a nearby garden.

We carefully covered our Savior's body with pounds of different spices. Then we wrapped Him in a long piece of fine linen cloth. It was hard work, and expensive, but I can afford it. My family's always been wealthy. It's time I used that money to care for people other than myself. Let Jesus benefit from it.

After Nicodemus and I prepared Jesus' body, several of us rolled a large stone in front of the cave-like tomb. Mary Magdalene and the other Mary are also here. They too are grieving and finding it hard to say goodbye to Jesus. Everyone else has gone; to where, I'm not sure. A strange darkness settled over Jerusalem while Jesus died. My heart feels the same way: uneasy, cold, and dark. We'll have to go home soon. The sun is setting, so we will observe the Sabbath and rest.

Today my love for Jesus gave me the courage to do what was right. I pray that, from now on, my words will be as honest and bold as my actions. No more hiding my faith in the dark.

Who showed bravery the day Jesus died?

Is there something you'd like to ask God to give you the courage to do?

Are you afraid to let your friends know you believe in Jesus? Why or why not?

19
Mary, Jesus' Mother

Ever since I was a little girl, I wanted to be a mother—to have children of my own. When an angel told me I was going to have a baby and that baby was going to be God's Son, I knew my life wasn't going to look like the one I'd always imagined. But then Jesus was born. He's been a wonderful Son. I'm not sure how I will live without Him.

So many people love Him, not just me. Young, old, men, women, children … they all followed Him, hanging on every word He said. I know the Jewish priests were jealous. That's why they wanted Him to die. But I also trust God's plan that the angel told me. That means I need to go on living … and loving … and waiting to see what God is going to do next, even though my heart is broken.

As a mother, I know that no one will ever take the place of my Son. Yes, I have other children. Even though they're grown, I'll always love and care for them as only a mother can. But for as long as I live, my Son Jesus will remain close. I'll always be thinking of Him, loving Him, missing Him …

Do you know that even while my Son—my special Son—was suffering on the cross, He was thinking of me? He told John, one of His followers and closest friends, to take care of me, to love me as if I were his very own mother. And Jesus asked me to care for John as if he were my very own son. Jesus knew that John and I needed each other. He also knew that we would do anything He asked. So we'll care for each other as family, in Jesus' name. We'll talk together about everything Jesus did and said and how much He meant to us.

Most importantly, we'll tell others how much He and His love changed our lives. We'll grieve together, and hopefully, one day, we'll smile together again too. I know that's what Jesus would want for all of us.

What do you think Mary was like as a mother?

How does God provide for you when you're hurting?

How do you now feel about Jesus, knowing He loved His mother so much?

20

Stone outside the Tomb

It's not often that a stone as big as I am gets to travel. Even if it *is* only a few feet. That's why I take my job so seriously. It's a privilege for an old limestone boulder like me to be rolled in front of a tomb, to stand guard over the body of a person who once walked freely on this earth. So when the people placed me here right before sunset a couple of days ago, I stood firm: tall and proud.

When Roman soldiers showed up, I admit I was surprised. They took turns standing guard right in front of me—all night, then all day, then all night again. Where did they think I was going? It had taken several men to put me here; it's not like I could easily be pushed aside.

The soldiers on duty weren't supposed to sleep, so they leaned up against me and talked about the dead man in the tomb behind me. They said His followers might try to steal His body. Then they laughed with each other, talking about rumors that the dead man inside might come back to life. If a stone could laugh, I would have joined them. After all, I've been around since the creation of the earth and had never seen or heard of such a thing.

Until this morning, that is …

What I remember most is the light! It was still early, and the first rays of sunshine hadn't yet begun to touch my stone-cold face. This light was coming from inside the tomb! Honestly, if the sky were filled with one hundred suns, it couldn't compare to the brilliant beam that warmly filled that dark cave where the man's body had been lovingly laid.

Unexpectedly, I began to tremble and roll. There was an earthquake, but that wasn't what moved me. It also wasn't a human hand. It was something else—something strong, yet gentle. I came to rest a few feet away from the mouth of the cave, feeling as light and nimble as a pebble.

Some of the guards fled screaming, leaving one behind with his mouth wide open, sitting still as a stone, looking as though he'd died of fright. What really happened this morning? I'm not sure. All I know is that now the tomb is empty—and I'm one bewildered boulder.

What makes rocks so interesting? What can we learn from them?

If you were one of the soldiers on guard that morning, what would you think? What would you tell people?

Why do you think the stone was moved?

Mary Magdalene

I know you may not believe what I'm going to tell you. Even Jesus' disciples didn't—at first. But listen! What I've seen and heard with my own eyes and ears is so incredible, I have to share it! After so many days of sadness, darkness, and death, this is the most incredible news!

This morning, Mary (James' mother), Salome, and I went to the tomb where Joseph and Nicodemus had laid Jesus' body a few days ago. We'd brought spices, which is our custom to honor the dead. Our hearts were so heavy. We wanted to do this for our dear friend Jesus, but how we would move the heavy stone that had been placed over the entrance, we had no idea.

As we neared the garden, I felt as though I were drowning in grief, and I again began to worry. Everything seemed hopeless. But when we arrived, the tomb was not only open but empty! Only the linen cloth that had wrapped Jesus' dead body remained. I panicked. My only thought was that someone must have stolen my Lord's body!

I ran back to tell the disciples that Jesus was gone. At least Peter and John listened to me. We hurried together to the tomb. They were faster than I was, and by the time I arrived, they'd already come and gone. There I stood, grieving at the empty tomb a second time. After Jesus died, all I had left of the Lord I loved was His body. Cruelly, now even that was gone. It felt as though my tears would never stop.

Then I heard a gentle voice asking why I was crying. My eyes were so swollen from all my crying that when I looked up, I could barely see. I figured the man half hidden in the early-morning shadows must be the gardener. I laugh at myself now, thinking about how wrong I was. As soon as the man called me by name, I knew it was Jesus Himself. I'd recognize the voice of my Lord anywhere, even from beyond the grave!

I was feeling so many emotions at once … shock, wonder, hope, and then joy! Jesus is alive! He has risen from the dead! I wanted to hold onto Him and never let go, but Jesus told me to hurry and tell His followers that the unbelievable has happened. That's why I'm telling you! Every word I've said is true. You must believe me: He's alive! Our Lord lives!

Why was Mary sad when she first went to Jesus' tomb?

If you were with Mary that morning, what would you think at first?

How can you celebrate the empty tomb?

22

Followers on the Road

This story may sound incredible, but my friend and I just saw and spoke with Jesus! He's alive!

It happened while we were coming down the road from Jerusalem to the little village called Emmaus. I was traveling with my friend Cleopas. The two of us were walking along and reflecting on all the terrible events that had just happened in Jerusalem. It had been three days since Jesus was buried, and we were both discouraged. The fresh air and quiet of the countryside allowed us to breathe again, but we couldn't stop thinking about what we had been through.

As we continued, a stranger joined us and asked what we were talking about. We looked at each other in surprise. Cleopas scoffed and asked how it was possible the man hadn't heard the news. The man genuinely seemed uninformed, so Cleopas related all that had taken place in recent days.

He described Jesus' trial and execution, even though all His disciples had expected Him to save Israel. Then there were the women who claimed to have seen Jesus at the tomb. He told the man how some of the disciples went to see the tomb for themselves but couldn't find Jesus' body anywhere. As I listened to Cleopas recount the events, I felt even sadder and more confused than before.

When he finished, the traveler slowly shook His head. He asked us why we didn't believe what the prophets had written about the promised Savior. The man began to explain how the Scriptures had foretold the Messiah's suffering and death and that it was all part of God's plan for His people. As I listened to the man—who was actually teaching us—I began to feel strangely calm and comforted.

When we finally arrived at our destination, we invited Him to join us for supper. As we sat down, He praised God and gave thanks for the food. Suddenly—and this is hard to explain—it was like a cloud was lifted from my eyes. I recognized who the man was: Jesus! Then He disappeared from the room!

Cleopas and I couldn't believe it! Immediately, we got up from the table to return to Jerusalem. We had to tell the disciples that we had seen Jesus living again. They had to know the good news: Jesus has risen from the dead, just as He said He would!

If you were with the men on the road, what would you tell Jesus?

Why do you think Jesus waited to reveal Himself to His followers?

What was the good news they rushed back to Jerusalem to share?

Thomas

My name is Thomas. Just Thomas. Please don't call me Doubting Thomas, like some people have started to do. That's a nickname I don't think I deserve! Ask anyone who knows me well. They'll tell you I've never been a person who goes along with the crowd just to fit in. Peer pressure doesn't work on me. I don't believe something just because someone else has told me it's true. I want proof.

That's why, when my ten friends, all close followers of Jesus, told me the Lord had appeared to them—after He'd died and been buried—well, that was something I had to see for myself. I told them that unless I could touch the marks from the nails on Jesus' hands and the wound where the soldier's spear had pierced His side, I wouldn't believe He'd risen from the dead. But, as always, my friend Jesus knew exactly how to help me believe in things that seem impossible …

About a week after my friends told me they'd seen Jesus, we were gathered together, talking, eating, and praying, like friends do. Then Jesus appeared right there with us! Did I mention all the doors in the room were locked? But suddenly, there He was, as alive as you and me. Jesus stood right in front of me and invited me to touch the wounds on His hands and side.

I fell to my knees and cried out, "My Lord and my God!" (John 20:28). I couldn't raise my head, let alone my hands. I didn't need to touch Him. I didn't need anything more than the presence of the Lord right by my side. Jesus wasn't upset that I hadn't believed what the other disciples had said; He is too full of love. But He did say that people who don't have the chance to see Him, yet still believe in Him, would be blessed.

I'm blessed too! I know for sure my Lord is alive. And there's more good news: Jesus promised that His Spirit would remain close to anyone who has faith in Him—as close to them as He was to me in that locked room. From now on, I'll never doubt my Lord is with me. I know He's always by my side—even when I can't see Him!

What's something you can't see but you know is real?

How would seeing Jesus in person change how you feel about Him?

How did Jesus feel about Thomas? How do you think Jesus feels about you—questions and all?

24

John

Here I am, right back where it all started. It feels like forever since I was just another fisherman working on the Sea of Galilee. But it's been three years since I left my nets behind to follow Jesus. That day, I never could have imagined how much that one decision would change my whole life.

Even though I'm home again, it doesn't feel the same. And I'm not really sure what happens next. At our Passover supper a few weeks ago, Jesus told us to meet Him in Galilee—after He rose from the dead! That night, we weren't sure what He meant. But a lot has happened since then. So here we are, in Galilee. Waiting.

This morning, before the sun came up, seven of us decided to head out and fish. We had to do *something*. Unfortunately, nothing was biting besides the mosquitoes. Then, as we were bobbing in the gentle waves, each deep in his own thoughts, a man onshore called out to us. He told us to throw our net on the other side of the boat. Why not? As soon as we did, so many fish swam into our net that our boat tilted to one side. It almost seemed like … a miracle! I'd seen this before!

Glancing back at the man on the beach, I knew … I just knew it was Jesus, my Lord and my friend! So did Peter. He jumped right into the water and began swimming to shore. The rest of us struggled to get all the fish we'd caught into the boat. Then we rowed as fast as we could to Jesus. He'd built a fire on the beach and cooked up some of the most amazing fish for breakfast. Leave it to Jesus to know just what we needed.

For years Jesus fed our minds with His words and our hearts with His love. This morning He's feeding our bodies with fish! I wish every person on earth could feel the joy of knowing Jesus the way I do. Maybe I should write everything down, record what Jesus has said and done, so none of what's happened will ever be forgotten. Like all those fish in the net, my mind is overflowing with so many wonderful stories! I can't wait to share them with the world!

What do you do when you're missing someone?

Why do you think Jesus made His friends breakfast?

Why do you think John wanted to write down everything he could remember about what Jesus had done?

25
Peter

Looking back at everything I've done, I'm still amazed: Jesus chose to forgive me.

I'll never forget the day Jesus called me to be His disciple. For the first time in my life, I felt like God was going to use me for something greater than myself. I followed Jesus everywhere, and I witnessed incredible miracles. I told Him I would follow Him even to death, but Jesus knew me better than I knew myself. He told me I would deny Him three times in a single night. I didn't believe I could do such a thing, but He was right. That same night, we celebrated the Passover together; then they arrested Him, and I denied I even knew Him. I didn't deserve to even look at Jesus, let alone speak to Him as His disciple.

Thankfully, the Lord had other plans for me.

Shortly after witnessing Jesus' crucifixion and the miracle of His resurrection, I returned to work as a fisherman—the only life I had known before being His disciple. It was early in the morning, and none of us had caught a single fish all night …

Until a man called out to us from the shore. He told us to throw our net over the other side of the boat. This command sounded familiar, so we obeyed. Immediately, we began pulling in more fish than our tiny boat could carry! Then John pointed to the man, recognizing Him as our Lord. I was so excited to see Jesus that I jumped into the water and swam to shore. Not only was it Him, but He had also prepared breakfast over a fire and was waiting for us. We sat down together to share a meal, like we used to.

When we were finished eating, Jesus and I took a walk. He asked me three times if I loved Him. It took me a while, but eventually, I realized what He was doing. This was Jesus' way of forgiving me for turning my back on Him.

Jesus had told me a while ago that I would be the rock on which He would build a strong church. I'm thankful that the Lord still has plans to use me to further His kingdom!

Since then, Jesus has returned to heaven. Even though He is no longer physically with us, we now have His Holy Spirit. Through each of us, the Lord is going to accomplish amazing things for His glory!

How can you show the love of Jesus to your friends?

How does it feel when someone forgives you for something you did wrong?

What do you think God might do in your life for His glory?

Why Did Jesus Die on the Cross?

God created everything—from the stars to the bugs—and it was good. The first two people, Adam and Eve, lived in a beautiful garden. They knew God very well and were close to Him.

But … Satan is a destroyer, so he lied to Adam and Eve. They didn't obey God, and their sin of disobedience broke the relationship they enjoyed with God. They could no longer be as close because He is holy.

This made God very sad. He made a plan to one day bring them back into relationship with Him because He loved them so much! He would send a Redeemer to save them by showing them how to restore their relationship.

Through the years and years and years, God showed who He was in the promises He made—and kept—in the lives of His people:

Noah …
Abraham …
Ruth …
Daniel …

Rahab …

and King David.

After so many years, it was time to send this Redeemer who would save people from their sins. He wanted people to decide to stop sinning and follow Him.

God sent His Son, Jesus, to earth both to be God and to live as a human. God wanted people to understand who He is through the words and actions of His Son.

Jesus was born as a baby to two regular people, Mary and Joseph, in a not-so-regular way. He came as a helpless baby and not a full-grown person. By letting people care for Him, He showed how humble He was. He also learned about all the things we go through. His miraculous birth was the first of many ways God showed His great love for us, the people He created.

When Jesus grew up, He showed God's love for us in the way He treated people, the lessons He taught, and the miracles He performed. Jesus cared for everyone He met and shared His message of how much God loves us.

Jesus invited people to trust in Him, then follow Him in the way they live their lives. He would save people from their sins and restore their relationship with God. But not everyone believed Jesus was God's Son, and some hated Him.

Then … Jesus allowed Himself to be sacrificed on a cross for our sins. He died so we can be close to God again. Someone had to pay the price for our sins, and Jesus was willing. That was God's plan all along. That's why Jesus died on the cross.

Jesus' friends and followers were very sad, but He didn't stay dead! On the third day, He came back to life. He is alive today and is living in heaven. By His Spirit, He lives within people who trust in Him.

We can know we will live forever in heaven with Jesus when our life on earth is done, if we accept Him as our Savior and Redeemer.

That's why God sent Jesus as a baby—for you and me.

That's why Jesus died on the cross—for you and me.

Note to Adults

We hope you've enjoyed experiencing the story of Jesus' resurrection through these twenty-five perspectives. Children already feel awe and wonder on a deep level. When we consider this familiar story—at least, familiar to us as adults—through their eyes and the viewpoints of the other witnesses to the miracle, our own sense of curiosity and the miraculous is restored.

If you would like to continue exploring these stories, there are numerous *The Action Bible* resources geared to the ages of your children:

The Action Storybook Bible: ages 4–8
The Action Bible Christmas: ages 5 and up
The Action Bible: Heroes and Villains: ages 8 and up
The Action Bible Anytime Devotions: ages 8 and up
The Action Bible Study Bible ESV: ages 8 and up

For even more *The Action Bible* resources, go to TheActionBible.com.

Additionally, the entire Easter story can be found in the Bible in Matthew 26–28; Mark 14–16; Luke 22–24; and John 18–21.

HERO or VILLAIN?
YOU DECIDE!

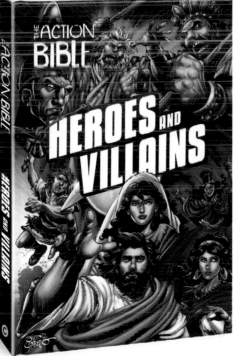